EMPATHS

Step-by-Step Guide for Highly Sensitive People

Lena Lind & Peter Harris

Contents

CHAPTER 1
I'M AN EMPATH

Has anyone ever said "you have a trusting face?" Do you find yourself listening with ease to other people's problems? Do strangers easily share intimate secrets? If so, you probably have gone through life being more affected by other peoples' energies than you realize.

As an empath, you are someone who has been hard-wired, from birth, to perceive and experience the thoughts, emotions, physical sensitivities, and spiritual urges of other persons. It is much more than being a highly sensitive person, and not limited to just emotions. For you, it can be like living an episode of Star Trek! You don't even have to try and you just know the motivations and intentions of other people.

You cannot change the fact that you are an empath. It is akin to your eye color. You either are or you're not. Being an empath is not teachable; it's not something to learn. However, you can learn to become a skilled empath and manage your empath nature. Hopefully you have, or will now, make it your intention to modify the intensity of the empath experience through adaptive means (meditation, movement, grounding, wearing protective stones). However, it is quite common for empaths to modify the feelings through not-so-adaptive means (alcohol, drugs, addictions). If you fall into that category, it is completely understandable and you are not alone!

The definition of being an empath means you are always "on," constantly available to process other people's feelings and energy. As an empath, you have a gift, or in many cases, what may feel like a serious curse! For now, let's set aside any notions of judgment. Even if it feels like an overwhelming burden, which it certainly is at times, our responsibility as an empath is to ourselves first, others second. So with that in mind, let's focus on how we can take responsibility for managing our energetic sensitivity.

Beware, though. Identifying and recognizing yourself as an empath may give you a charge. It may cause lingering sensations of relief, bordering on giddiness. You will come to understand that as an empath you are not alone.

So with that in mind, let's talk about some of the most helpful methods of keeping yourself clean, strong, and healthy as an empath, free of the negative energetic influences of others.

1. Reframe Your Mental Outlook

Being an empath is indeed a burden at times. To be maximally effective, we must do what counselors call reframing, that is, changing our mental outlook so there is no room for blame. We can do very little to change our currently inherited genetic characteristics.

As empaths, it is helpful to take a close look at our personal narrative. What are the stories that we tell ourselves as we wash dishes or peel potatoes? If we believe in a story that we need protection from evil spirits or negative energy, then we more likely set ourselves up for the manifesting of that scenario. As empaths, we understand what's it's like to be knocked around by other people's energy. However, I don't think that it's maximally effective to focus on just protection.

If we focus instead on how to maintain a strong healthy aura, any negative energies will be naturally and automatically dispelled. Negative energy cannot exist in the presence of light. To use a sports or political metaphor, it's a question of whether you want to be on offense or defense. Focusing on promoting positive strengths is almost always more effective than a mental outlook that's designed to protect your empath energy from invasion. That said it is absolutely true that empaths need protection - we just don't want to overdo it.

2. Use Protecting Stones And Wear A Medicine Kit

Stones have been known for their healing and protective properties for thousands of years. Stones are the oldest material on the earth; they are living creatures who offer their medicine to us if we will use it. Stones can be worn by carrying a medicine pouch around your neck or by wearing stone jewelry. The three best repellants for negative energy are Tourmaline, Onyx and Obsidian. Just like you, your stones must be cleaned regularly. Give your stones at least 2-

3 hours of direct sunlight in a crystal or glass bowl filled with sea salt and water. If you can't get access to sunlight, run them under some tap water. It does almost as good a job.

3. Move!

Exercise and movement in any form are great ways for empaths to move out old energy and pull in fresh energy. Martial arts and yoga are two of the best methods for an empath. Even a simple movement of one's arm might be enough, or even a simple acknowledgment that your wrist hurts. The body responds to our focused attention in-kind. If you are intimidated by the concept of martial arts, then try yoga, Tai Chi, Qi Gong, or a user-friendly practice such as Nia, which is now emerging worldwide.

4. Program your brain with affirmations and prayer.

Actual physical voicing of particular words and sounds produce a powerful effect in our empath energy fields. This is known as Neuro-linguistic programming. The brain and body are programmed to produce good feelings with the repeating of certain mantras, words, or phrases. The process is designed to stimulate the empath nervous system into intentionally producing the actual energetic vibrations and feelings of peace, happiness, joy, and tranquility.

When you become a conscious empath, you will dramatically reduce your stress and anxiety, improve your mental outlook, improve relationships, and lead to a freedom and liberation previously unknown. You will be able to create joy where none was before present. In situations where you previously felt trapped, you now can bring in positive energy to change situations.

You'll begin to light up other people's lives in a new way, and fulfill your destiny as an empath to help others. All of these skills take practice. With time, they will come more naturally. At some point, you will reach a tipping point; a critical point where your awareness exceeds your unconsciousness. It takes work on yourself to get to this place.

Some empaths go all their lives and never reach it, but only for lack of will. If your will is strong enough, you will reach a place of emotional maturity and become a skilled empath.

CHARACTERISTICS OF AN EMPATH

Empaths are loving; caring, kind people who want to help others. They are often found doing volunteer work and may serve others through emotionally-demanding careers as childcare givers, medical professionals, hospice workers, midwives, and such. Most empaths came in with a mission to heal people, animals, plants, and the planet. As healers, many have taken on so much external energy that they spend most of their time trying to clear unwanted energy and recuperate from the last episode that "blew their doors off."

Here are a few characteristics of empaths who have not learned to filter out other people's emotions or manage their own energy:

- You constantly feel overwhelmed with emotions and you may cry a lot, feel sad, angry, or depressed for no good reason. You may be tempted to think you are crazy for having random mood swings and bouts of unexplained fatigue. If you are a woman, it's like having PMS all the time! Unrestrained empathy can cause a person to manifest symptoms similar to bipolar (manic-depressive) disorder.

- You drop by the store feeling great, but once you get in a crowd you start feeling down, angry, sad, or overwhelmed. You feel you must be coming down with something so you decide to go home and rest.

- If you've found that you can't be in public without becoming overwhelmed you may start to live the life of a hermit. But, even at home, you get depressed when you watch the news and you cry while watching a movie. You feel horrible when a commercial for the Humane Society shows animals that need a home. You may rescue more animals than you can possibly care for.

- You feel sorry for people no matter who they are or what they have done. You feel the need to stop and help anyone in your path. You can't pass by a homeless person without giving him money-even if you don't have it to spare.

- Many empaths are overweight. When they absorb stressful emotions, it can trigger panic attacks, depression as well as food, sex, and drug binges. Some may overeat to cope with emotional stress or use their body weight as a shield or buffer. In Chapter 9 of Yvonne Perry's book, she shows how to use light as protection.

- Most empaths have the ability to physically and emotionally heal others by drawing the pain or ailment out of the sick person and into their own bodies. For obvious reasons, this is not recommended unless you know how to keep from becoming ill in the process.

- From chest pains and stomach cramps to migraines and fever, you manifest symptoms without contracting an actual illness. Later, you learn that your "ailment" coincided with the onset of a friend or family member's illness.

- No one can lie to you because you can see through their face and know what they really mean. You may even know why they lied.

- People-even strangers-open up and start volunteering their personal information. You may be sitting in the waiting room minding your own business and waiting your turn when the person next to you starts sharing all kinds of personal information. You didn't ask them to and they never considered that you might not want to hear about their drama. People may feel better after speaking with you, but you end up feeling worse because they have transferred their emotional pain to you.

- Some empaths don't do well with intimate relationships. Constantly taking on their partner's pain and emotions, they may easily get their feelings hurt, desire to spend time alone rather than with the partner, feel vulnerable when having sex, and feel that they have to continually retrieve their own energy when it gets jumbled with that of their partner. They may be so afraid of becoming engulfed by another person that they close up emotionally just to survive.

- The ill, the suffering, and those with weak boundaries are drawn to the unconditional understanding and compassion an empath emits without even being aware of it. Until you learn how to shut out the energy of others, you may have a pretty miserable existence in which you feel like you have to be entirely alone in order to survive.

It's easy to see why being an empath is often very draining. No wonder that over time, some folks shut down their empathic ability. And, with that, they also shut down a vital part of their divine guidance system. Learn how to manage the amount of info-energy you receive and hear more of what is really important.

THINGS THAT MIGHT MEAN YOU ARE AN EMPATH

Being an empathic person can be challenging. Many Empaths have no idea why they feel overwhelmed by life. Their families are critical and call them too sensitive or recluse. This gift of sensitivity isn't a bad trait but something that can be controlled and should be celebrated.

An Empath receives more information about the world and activities than those who scoff at them. While it may be hard to process all the energetic information being received, an Empath can do wondrous things with this way of sensing life. Here are 20 things commonly experienced by Empaths. If your life is like this, you just might be an Empath too.

- You can walk past a crowd of people and start to feel strange. You may suddenly feel angry or sad. The emotion overwhelms you and you just have to get away. You have no explanation for your sudden changes in emotions. You just FEEL it.

- You've been called overly sensitive all your life and usually in a negative connotation, but you know it isn't you, it's the surroundings.

- You experience others physical ailments. Someone in the room has a headache and after entering the room, you do too. You were fine before entering the room. This frequently happens to people you have relationships with, but it can occur with anyone.

- You feel so lethargic that you just stay in bed. It isn't depression, but you would just rather be alone. You aren't a loner; you just need to be alone to recharge your battery. When company leaves, you need a nap.

- Your fatigue coincides with a family member's illness, but you live in another state and there has been no communication between the two of you prior to your fatigue.

- You are overwhelmed when watching horrible thing that happen in real life or on television. Do you experience the feelings of the people involved as though you've been punched in the gut or burst into tears, shaking etc?

- You can drive over a place where there has been an accident and suddenly crumple in physical or emotional pain.

- You aren't able to watch the news.

- You always know what someone really means and what they really meant to say.

- You always know when someone is lying. I've always called this my BS Meter.

- You have a knowing about situations that is more than intuition, hunches or statistical probability.

- You feel compelled to care for someone even if they are unkind to you.

- You feel compelled to care for someone on the spot and generally that help is accepted.

- People tell you their life story and wonder why they are telling you all about it.

- You can't stand In Your Face people and just want to stay away from them and generally be alone. You are very sensitive to smells, excessive talking or loud sounds. You may be so overwhelmed that you develop physical symptoms like headaches, or instant colds.

- You have the ability to heal instinctively by drawing pain or ailments into your own body.

- You would rather drive in your own car, so that you can get out quickly when you start to feel overloaded.

- You often feel spacey and clumsy because all the incoming energies unground you.

This list of list of possible behaviors can help you decide if you are an Empath or not. If you do feel like you are an Empath, you probably need help working with all the energy and information coming at you. Look for ways to deal with it all and you'll find like a kinder place to be.

CHAPTER 2

EMPATHIC ABILITIES

It is sometimes hard to tell whether or not someone is an empath, (a psychic who possesses empathic abilities). The problem is you don't always know if someone actually possesses these psychic powers, or if they are just sensitive, understanding people. How do you know if you're really empathic?

Empaths are extremely sensitive to the feelings of those around them. Often, an empath will be able to sense what someone is experiencing, even if they can't see or hear that person. Someone with this kind of ability simply "knows." Many psychics with empathic abilities report experiencing someone else's feelings as though they were their own, though this is not always the case.

A psychic with this kind of ability will be able to sense the feelings of others, especially if those feelings are very strong. Common feelings that an empath will experience include fear, joy, loneliness, excitement, love, and foreboding. The stronger the feelings, the easier it will be for the empath to sense, understand, and feel.

The thing that sets empaths apart from other, "normal" people is that they have a deeper, more sensitive understanding for what they are feeling. This intuition comes from within, and is far greater than what most people experience. For example, a "normal" person might realize that someone they love is upset by little things they say or do.

However, an empath would sense this even without seeing or talking to that person and an empath could sense if that loved one was feeling betrayed, jealous, angry, or hurt. This psychic intuition would come from within, not from the visual or audible clues of the physical world.

Empaths are able to tell when something is wrong, even if that something hasn't happened yet. They are overcome with a deep sense of foreboding that warns them that everything is not as it should be. A "normal" person, on the other hand, would not be able to tell when something unexpected or dangerous was going to happen.

These things all sound great, but not everyone realizes that it can also be very difficult to be an empath. This is because empaths are not able to "shut off" their abilities whenever they want. That is, they cannot choose whether or not to feel something. Instead, they must feel whatever their psychic intuition senses, even if they would rather not. This is a huge burden for empaths, and it is also why empathic psychics can get sick from exhaustion.

PSYCHIC READINGS - UNDERSTANDING THE PSYCHIC EMPATH

One of the most common forms of psychic ability is that of the Psychic Empath. Psychic Empaths are individuals that can sense or feel the emotions of others. They can also experience the same emotions or sensations that someone else is experiencing. Their true gift lies in their unique ability to focus on the energy or emotions that are influencing people. They also have the psychic aptitude to tune into one's spiritual guides. In essence, they are messengers. Not only can they deliver information from the spiritual realm, they can also help by interpreting ones inner, emotional states.

To some degree, we are all Empaths. The more in tune we are with our own emotions, the easier it is to tune into the emotions of others. The most common problem that occurs, however, is when we find ourselves overly identified with other people. Psychic Empaths often struggle with this. For the Psychic Empath, a great deal of self-care is needed. The gift of the Psychic Empath can be a difficult one. They constantly have to protect themselves by setting appropriate boundaries with their subjects.

Take for example, the individual that recently experienced the death of a close one. The Psychic Empath will experience the same grief, sadness and anger as the individual who has just lost their loved one. The Psychic Empath must develop the appropriate skills to shield themselves from taking this on. They must learn to separate their own emotions from their subjects.

The Psychic Empath can learn to do this through a number of techniques. The most popular technique is through a grounding meditation. This is a type of mediation in which the Empath spiritually, emotionally, and visually connects themselves to the earth. It enables them to ground their body and mind to the power of the earth. This connection can keep the Empath in their own body and protects them from losing themselves in the realm of emotions.

Another popular technique is that of a protection meditation. A protection meditation includes the sensing or visualization of a protective divine light. The Empath uses this divine light as a barrier between their own emotions and that of their subjects. Although they still can experience the emotions of others, they are protected against "taking on" the emotions of others.

A gifted Empath can provide powerful psychic readings. They are particularly skilled at connecting to their subject's guides, angels, or deceased loved ones. If you are experiencing an abundance of negative or overwhelming emotions, a Psychic Empath can help you work through these.

They are there to help you to discover what may be influencing your emotions and provide you with the necessary solutions to process them. They can also deliver important messages from the spirit world, often providing the insight to help you grow as an individual.

CHAPTER 3

HOW TO ACHIEVE SPIRITUAL AWAKENING

Have you met an Indian Guru or Buddhist Monk before? Many of us have never encountered such a person. All we really know about them is what we see in images or as a Hollywood interpretation. It is quite easy to say they might have a dreamy or blissful look and manner. It is this manner you may wish to achieve with a spiritual awakening, but first you must divest yourself of the mundane. A lot of us live in busy cities with stress as our main meal. It is a life of deadlines, expectations and high goals that will dominate our lives.

You will most likely have an urge to rid yourself of these worries and thoughts every once in a while, but the question of how to achieve this will be foremost in your mind.

Will traveling to a resort, playing in your garden, or any other method of peaceful activity really restore you and reduce the stress? The answer is probably not. Instead you need a spiritual awakening that will cure what ails you.

So what is this spiritual awakening we are discussing? A spiritual awakening is a process that helps an individual become balanced. It is meant to increase your awareness, offer enlightenment, and above all transcend you into another plane. The question now becomes how you will enter this state of being? Do you have to become a monk or recluse to concentrate on your "rebirth"? Some might find it helpful, but it is actually quite a detailed process you have to follow.

Meditation and Spiritual Awakening

To bring about a spiritual awakening you need to understand how your mind works. You need to know what is tangible, what is intangible and then understand that we are all a product of our mind and process. Only a portion of our brain is ever used until a spiritual awakening occurs in which we can interpret things in a different light. We can no longer depend on our perception as a truth because it is always filtered by the mind and what we have been told to perceive.

We have been told the color blue is actually blue, but couldn't it have been called red and we would have the same perception? The fact is those who believe in spiritualism and its awakening in the human body believe that color is an illusion because our minds are interpreting it for us in its limited capacity. You must try to relax and concentrate in order to reach a spiritual awakening.

Try to imagine a dome that is invisible to sight and that your mind is outside of this dome. It is a place where thoughts and fantasy are not able to go. If you can reach this state you will find silence in which your mind will be free. You will have feelings of an encompassing nature. Your body and mind will be enlightened where you will have a good hold on reality rather than false images and perception. Peace will enter you.

Practice Required

Practice is required to achieve a state of spiritual awakening within yourself. As long as you can practice you can continue to be at peace and in balance.

KUNDALINI - A SPIRITUAL AWAKENING

There are many different views on the Kundalini awakening process and also many differing experiences. Some say that awakening Kundalini can lead to insanity, others that it leads to enlightenment, that it is our birthright and the next stage in human evolution. I believe it is the latter but in some ways both are correct. When Kundalini is awakened it does lead to an insanity of sorts, a loss of one's mind, or ego.

As all the experiences of our life come flooding back to us and our awareness grows beyond anything we could have previously imagined, it may feel like we are going insane, losing our mind, but in reality we are actually becoming sane, breaking free from our conditioned, linear ways of thinking, free to see and experience the universe for what it truly is. A huge shift in our perspective occurs, and we become able to see the connectedness of all things and to realize our true nature and full potential.

As the process unfolds the outer layers of our selves are peeled away, bit by bit, until our true self emerges, clear of all past karma and emotional blockages. A metamorphosis that happens from the inside out. Releasing and healing any traumas that are still being held inside the body and consciousness. The reason why some are classed as insane or develop psychological problems is because they are trying to stop or suppress the process through traditional methods and without a proper understanding of what is occurring.

Kundalini cleanses the soul, the mind and the physical body and it is normal to experience some sort of psychological disturbance and possibly physical disturbance. But you must allow Kundalini to do what it has to do, surrender to it, do not put up resistance as this will only make the experience more uncomfortable and traumatic.

Do not be afraid of it, welcome and nurture it and the process will unfold in a much more harmonious way. Learn all you can about Kundalini. Look at differing views and make up your own mind, find your own truth. No one can tell you what is right and what is not, the truth lies within you, the knowledge is there already, you just have to remember.

There are certain methods and techniques which you can use yourself to awaken Kundalini, including certain types of meditation and breathing techniques. But be aware, once you start on this path, there is no going back, as those who awaken Kundalini and then try to suppress it are bound to experience problems.

Some advise that Kundalini must be awakened by a 'Master' or 'Guru'; this is your choice and is totally dependent on your own level of Spiritual development, personal knowledge, understanding and belief system. If you choose to try and awaken it yourself then you should prepare your mind and body for what is in store, attempt to clear as many toxins from the body as possible, eat well, and avoid alcohol and recreational drugs as these can all hamper the process and can lead to problems.

Keep active, you must find ways of releasing excess energy otherwise it will become stagnant and could cause problems. A good way to combine physical activity with the process is through Kundalini Yoga which was specifically created to awaken Kundalini and is reported to be one of the earliest forms of yoga. It is similar to Hatha yoga but with more focus on awakening Kundalini. Ha-tha literally means Sun-Moon, and yoga means union, so a union of the sun and moon energies, which is what, occurs during the Kundalini awakening process.

It is important to read as much as possible about the process, but remember to find your own truth, do not rely on anyone else to tell what is right and what is not. Approached with the right attitude and with correct preparation Kundalini is an amazing, joyful experience.

If we go through this process with love, compassion and forgiveness in our hearts and embrace the process fully then it is truly the ultimate goal in our spiritual development, the true path to Enlightenment and an evolution of consciousness.

EMPATHS WORKING WITH ASCENDED MASTERS

Each embodied soul needs an anchor in higher realms of consciousness to stabilize the vibration of the physical body on Earth. Since we wear the vibrational frequencies of those we align with, naturally the purer those frequencies, the more enjoyable they are and the smoother goes our lives. Some people are now working with ascended masters to help the Earth and humanity shift into lighter planes of consciousness. They are receiving intense and pure energy in their bodies in order to anchor these frequencies in the Earth plane.

In allowing ascended masters to send pure frequencies of energy from cosmic, solar, and multidimensional sources, a number of fully-trained empaths are using their chakras and subtle bodies as channels similar to high-voltage transformers, which step down intensely vibrating frequencies into a more useable and less harmful current that can be accepted by humanity. However, this is causing some emotional, mental, and physical discomfort.

In addition to trying to heal their own past, these people may feel drained because they are also picking up negative energy from those around them in order to transmute it and free others from karma and suffering. Karma is the "law of sin and death" that the Bible mentions. It keeps us on a cycle of reincarnation, which is a very slow way to ascend. We are under the law of grace, which is freedom from guilt, shame, and punishment. We can live in experiential knowledge of this bliss and ascend more quickly and with less symptoms of resistance.

Many starseeds (souls who have been to other places before coming to Earth), walk-ins (souls that come into a mature body rather than being born into an infant), lightworkers (more evolved souls here to help the planet ascend), and indigos (children who possess unusual and/or supernatural traits or abilities) have agreed to come to Earth to perform certain duties.

Transmuting negativity into positive or beneficial energy is one of those tasks. Unfortunately, many empaths use their body for this purpose. Instead, you can establish a rapport with one or more ascended master and ask them to assist with helping you fulfill your divine purpose on Earth. They are more than willing to work with you and help you raise your own vibration so you are less affected by detrimental energy.

Some of you are using energy, light, and information to heal people, plants, animals, and the Earth's soil, air, and water. Some of you are serving as activists for social reform, humanitarian efforts, and better health/living conditions throughout the world.

Others have discovered a talent for writing and teaching, delivering channeled messages, or providing intuitive readings. Some are finding that they can influence the weather, align the earth's gridlines (ley lines), and do many other important spiritual tasks such as transmuting karma for others.

AN EMPATH VENTURE INTO HEALING

If you are sensitive you most likely know it about yourself in a very deep way. You feel energy easily and are an empath. Some empaths who takes classes in Healing/Universal Tao and other Internal Alchemy programs are learning to take one step at a time in feeling things.

Others are tending toward such sensitivity that your body is basically 'spinning' on the energy. The methods I am teaching simply pronounce them more clearly and loudly for your body/mind/HEART to react upon. Please don't tell yourself the feelings are "freaky" or give up too soon on the developmental process. Your monkey mind may lie and judge.

KNOW THIS and change your language usage: Tell yourself the truth about feeling energy is not to randomly come and go, but it'll become usable to you when you need it. It takes time to develop correctly! Even highest level healers can have times in their life when their energy is not of the most useful level, so naturally those who are just beginning cannot take for granted that strong feelings of healing force are always in the best of control. Students at all levels practice to become certain your abilities become consistently useful. Training sufficiently hones you to your best.

Adepts start feeling there is an extraordinary HEIGHTENING of energy feelings. It alerts people to possibly begin re-experiencing old illnesses. Someone may also be experiencing energetic symptoms as well as physical. If your nervous system has been heightened since childhood, this work enhances it more. It might do well for me as a teacher to tell all new students that all feelings that are new can feel overly pronounced and can seem temporally irritating.

Irritations will calm down in the same way that a dive into a pool of water calms down. The first dive one takes can for some feel like a shock, but many people subsequently love the feeling. Feeling the bliss of aroused energy without experiencing the overly sensationalized feelings that are more pronounced in the beginning is what you train to monitor through practice. You set your dials just right for YOU.

It is not easy for any diet, series of hypnosis, NLP or other programs that bring about changes in which you might have ever partaken during your sensitive lifetime to bring about a similar type of heightened sensation about which we are describing. But such things can happen. Your good intentions to heal and become a healer might feel that you walked through a door that is going to become a HOME for you that will eventually feel normal and comfortable, but for now, it is strange.

It only becomes stranger if you are not aware that you are heightening odd feelings if you become scared. (It may not be within the classes in Internal Alchemy Healing where you experienced this. There could be many other examples of such feelings that occur in situations apart from a classroom where a person is being taught techniques to become a more capable self healer or healer. Instantaneous and shocking spurts of energy are not so common. People don't often discuss them. Some people refer to such phenomenon as "Kundalini Syndrome" which has many diverse expressions in individuals.

When encountering an over load of energy, the first step is to smile. Do Inner Smile to your organs, with or without Healing Sounds. Move your Macrocosmic Orbit. Just sit, stand or lay down doing the techniques and know what you are doing is TAKING THE CONTROLS to guide your energy so that you can handle it. 'Temporarily over-heightened energy comes into your body similarly as putting too much voltage into an outlet'. Spiral the usable energy into your body and with the rest, it is also a good remedy to brush off your body of the 'things you don't need any more', which includes energy overload.

In our classes we throw the energy with our fingertips which have brushed down the center line of the body, into the earth. This is a well known Qigong balancing practice. You can even pat the ground a few times and strongly command the recycling to instantaneously begin! Energy in itself is a force that needs attention. Most important is that you calm yourself down and relax the tissues of the entire body which is done in Inner Smile and Orbit meditations.

As an empath, an unnerving experience of heightened energy has possibly had the chance to come to your attention. This sometimes can set off a modus operendi in a person. Perhaps a part of you felt that in the past or even currently, your fellow students in school, co-workers or family gave you feed back that was hinted at. You began to think that people see you as being a little 'off'. Don't forget that many other people see you as a loving, sweet and sensitive person. It is rarely everyone that agrees on negative stereotypes. Empaths are prone to letting your mind go too long in seeing yourself by others' more negative and stereotyping judgments.

It is time to take command and become, slowly and surely, the person who no longer allows negative people you know to be so rude as to be asking, as an example, "Are you on some downers?" Or "uppers" or whatever their own drug history would lead them to conclude! You can probably remember other digs someone might throw at you or another sensitive person. Such "disses", as they are now called, have shamefully become an accepted and too common behavior.) People don't even realize anymore that people who partake in such behavior are out of line in a way quite explainable; our society has modeled so much rude behavior in the media! 'Sensitives' are more likely to question themselves rather than others.

Do your best to know the fallacy of these jibes. Your own insecurities which have been wrongly branded into you through incorrect readings by others make it challenging to see that you are a power house of LOVE and there is abundant healing ability resident in your bones. Please don't let this scare you, but make you feel like the journey, (which needs lots of slow steps), is already a lovely one, even with misinterpretations that you or others might impose.

As a more extreme example of being jibed there are psychic attacks like witch craft and negative spiritual entities. These cannot enter a person who is constantly strengthening themselves by employing the energies and lights that are strengthened with constant practice, practice, practice of making them a tool that you can take out when you need them.

We don't call these practices, "Energy Medicine" for no reason. Western doctors are always learning new things and so are Eastern doctors. You are becoming an Artist and Scientist in one body!

Many an artist has ripped up a drawing and some writers have thrown out an entire novel. What scientist hasn't had many experiments go awry? Before any healing artist becomes secure in their work, things can appear distorted. Give yourselves plenty of time to grow. An evolution inside you is taking place.

That can also lead to megalomania where in which you think you have become powerful with little practice and haven't really digested the energy enough yet. You might become braggadocios and this is not what you are looking to do. (This is an opposite example to the rest and it happens often also.) Let yourself slowly evolve. Be in no hurry. Be secure. Be safe. Be gently self-nurturing. Have fun on your pathway to evolving yourself.

CHAPTER 4

A SURVIVAL GUIDE FOR EMPATHS AND HIGHLY SENSITIVE PERSONS

Empaths are very special people, and face multiple daily challenges. You connect with the energy of others sharing your space, and also your environment (through energy imprints). This can be overwhelming at times and in order to gain control and manage your own energy, a few tools can be essential. Here are some tips and techniques that have proven to be valuable assets for the empath's toolbox.

Positive affirmations are also very helpful. A positive affirmation is a short sentence or two that supports positive thought patterns and can actually re-train your brain. An example, let me receive what is in my best and highest good at this time, is both raising your energetic signature and open ended.

Why is open ended a good thing? It doesn't define which can sometimes place limits or expectations providing an unintended consequence. What is what is the best and highest good is better than you have imagined? If you leave it open ended, it can flow right to you. I enjoyed, Outrageous Openness by Tosha Silver, which did a wonderful job of breaking this down and giving more insight into how this works.

Shielding is another tool you can use when you are just getting started. This involves calling in a high vibrational energetic field to protect you. You can call in Angels and see them standing by you in your mind's eye, or imagining a white light encasing you.

Another method is to see yourself in armor made of mirrors which send energy right back to its source. A developed empath will be able to allow energy to flow through without absorbing any. This takes confidence and skill. You can develop this with practice. It is the knowledge that any energy that flows towards you is temporary, like a breeze. It can flow right through you. You can feel it, know it does not belong to you and allow it to pass through without absorbing any of it.

Good energetic hygiene is a must for any empath. It starts with a basic understanding of chakras, and then a simple visualization of cleansing them. Some people see the chakra wheels of color and imagine them spinning with bright healthy color and any dark spots of negativity are removed.

Doing this in the shower can be quite effective as any negativity goes right down the drain with the dirty bath water! You can also imagine white light coming in through your crown chakra, nourishing and replenishing the chakras.

Meditation and centering are also valuable assets for your empathic toolbox. Meditation for 10-20 daily will bring profound change. Centering involves coming back to self. Empaths connect with others and it's like an energetic handshake. Your energy goes out to meet and greet others, and centering brings you back into your body fully. This allows you to align with spirit/source energy and step out of ego. Mindfulness is great for centering. Try to live in the moment and whatever emotion comes up acknowledge, express and then release it.

Stones and essential oils can also be helpful. Depending on how you are wired you might prefer one more than the other. Remember you are an individual, your expression of empathic ability and empathic experience may be similar to another person's, however the truth is you are a unique divine expression. That means you will vibe strongly and have an affinity with some things and not others. That's your beauty and why the world needs you!

Forgiving others and forgiving self is one of the most powerful tools you have. It will clear your energy and raise your vibrational rate. Remember forgiveness is for your well-being the other person doesn't need "to forgive you" for benefit. It can be a challenge to do this, however it is necessary for your growth and evolution. No one has walked this earth and not harmed, intentionally or unintentionally, another being. It is part of the human experience. So like the prayer says... forgive others and forgive yourself.

The root chakra connects us to the earth. Be aware of this and using visualization ground into the earth. See (using your mind's eye) a cord connecting you to the earth. You can then use it to send negative energy into the earth where it is absorbed and to draw up nourishing energy from the center of the earth. Doing this will increase your energy flow.

Others helpful techniques include listening to music or nature sounds. Spending time in nature and with your pets is a great way to relax, clear your energy and center yourself. Exercise programs will support a good energetic flow. Yoga is really good because it combines breathing with poses that encourage alignment and flow of energy.

Keep your environment clear of negativity. Raise those vibes! The Native Americans' have been smudging with great results for years. Burning sage while stating an intention is a great method for clearing energy. In your office area you can use a spritzer bottle with water and salt, or make an aroma therapy spritzer.

If you use essential oils remember that oil and water don't mix so you'll want to add some witch hazel or alcohol to the water and oils. A cup of water, ¼ cup of witch hazel and 7-10 drops of oil. Journal the gratitude! Ending the day by writing a list of things you are grateful for in a journal and

then stating an intention or affirmation keeps the positive
energy flowing.

THE EMPATH BLUES: WAYS TO RELIEVE EMOTIONAL FATIGUE

According to Wikipedia, "decisional fatigue refers to the deteriorating quality of decisions made by an individual, after a long session of decision making". This concept has been studied extensively in psychology where people who have to make a lot of decisions as part of their daily job, like judges for example, become worn out over time and tend to make poorer decision later in the day. The mind becomes exhausted and has a hard time evaluating tradeoffs, a critical skill in decision making.

In a similar vein, Empaths can become overly activated by the constant emotional information that they have to process. This is especially true for Impaired Empaths who have a hard time regulating the influx of emotions they pick up from other people. Overtime, their ability to appropriately respond to emotions can become erratic, leaving them feeling powerless and depressed.

Under a spell of the Empath blues, you might start to feel sad without knowing why. You are also more likely to feel depressed later in the day, waking up fine in the morning but experiencing a decline in your positive emotions as the day goes by. The Empath blues is typically temporary but can become chronic if left unattended. Please note that anyone who feels depressed over a long period of time might be suffering from clinical depression and should immediate seek medical help as well as therapeutic counseling.

So what can you do when you find yourself in the throes of the Empath blues? There is a very common misconception that the remedy for emotional fatigue is to try to be "happier". Meaning that you should try to think positively, even though you feel utterly crappy. Have you ever been with someone who was trying to cheer you up while you felt sad? Despite their best efforts, you kind of want them to shut up and go away.

This reaction makes perfect sense when you consider that alleviating emotional fatigue requires emotional quiet, which is the absence of strong emotions. Feeling happy is a strong emotion and strong emotions, whether positive or negative, are exactly what caused emotional fatigue in the first place!

Not only that but trying to cheer up on the spot takes a huge amount of effort when you are feeling sad. You're trying to jump from one end of the emotional spectrum (sadness) into the opposite end (happiness) while being exhausted, so you're more likely to fall flat on your face mid jump.

Most Empaths are not familiar with the state of emotional quiet required to address emotional fatigue. They are so used to feel tugged in all kinds of emotional direction that feeling nothing is often equated with feeling dead or empty. They wonder if something's wrong. And yet, this is no different than sleep for the body! We need down time where we let out body, mind and emotions rest.

Fortunately, Empath are often very intuitive beings. They feel drawn to what is good for them. That's why if you're an Empath you'll probably recognize some of your own urges in the 4 most effective ways to relieve emotional fatigue.

Being alone: Empaths need time by themselves where they are less likely to be tuning into the emotions of others around them. It doesn't mean you're anti-social or that you don't like people! It just means you need to refuel before going back out into the world. Make sure you have plenty of alone time when you're doing something that is not emotional, such as knitting, gardening, cooking, etc.

Being in nature: Many Empaths report feeling most at peace in nature, among trees and in large bodies of water like the ocean or a lake. With good reasons! Trees and water provide a natural "white noise" when it comes to emotional vibration. It's like wearing a noise canceling headset to drown out the emotions of people.

Being physical active: Physical activity can provide a great buffer against emotional fatigue by taking your focus away from emotions and into your own physical body. For our purposes, the physical activity needs to be challenging enough that it requires your full attention. Rock climbing and yoga are my favorite activities to get emotionally quiet.

Meditation: Meditation provides a powerful way to guide your focus away from other people. This can be very challenging for Empaths who tend to always tune into others.

It can feel unnatural or difficult at first. But being able to create a quiet space within, whether by focusing on your breath or by following a guided audio meditation, can give you the space you need to rest both your mind and your delicate emotional system.

HOW TO PROTECT YOURSELF AGAINST ENERGY VAMPIRES

We all know at least one energy vampire. They might be perfectly nice, in fact, they generally are, but spending time with them leaves you feeling drained and weak. They complain to you about their lives, you commiserate with them. You so want to help them feel better and they often do after speaking with you. But at what cost? Is there a way to deal with these energy vampires, other than cutting them out of your life altogether? How can you protect yourself against other people "robbing" you of your energy?

First of all, it's important to understand exactly what is happening on an energetic level. No one can "rob" you of your energy. Your energy is not finite, and you can't give it away or take it from someone else.

Energy vampirism generally comes about when someone with a lower vibration seeks out someone with a higher vibration and uses them to raise their own vibration a bit - making them feel better in the process. The issue arises when the person with the higher vibration isn't stable in that frequency and allows the person with the lower vibration to influence them energetically.

If you're a person who's often been accused of being overly sensitive or empathetic, you're probably someone who is easily influenced by the energy around you. Don't worry, this doesn't mean that you're broken somehow. It just means that you never learned how to stabilize your vibration. And how could you have? The answer isn't to "just deal with it" or "grow up" as you might've been told. But it also means that you don't have to be at the mercy of the frequencies around you. You can definitely learn to hold your vibration, even when faced with an energy vampire.

If you're often sought out by others to make them feel better, chances are that your vibration is probably generally on the high side. You may allow yourself to be influenced, but you always eventually return to your naturally high vibration. You're probably quite positive and loving, and others naturally feel the good energy flowing off you. Again, this isn't a bad thing - you're a natural uplifter - unless, of course, you're faced with someone who begins to pull your vibration down.

Let's say that someone you care about is upset and wants to talk to you about it. Fair enough. You're a caring person, you love to help. This friend of yours begins to complain about her boss and what a jerk he is. Her work life is nothing but stress. She goes on and on about how horrible her colleagues are, the backstabbing that goes on, how depressing it all is and how she feels utterly helpless in her situation.

And what do you do? You listen intently, make soothing comments and you begin to empathize. You begin to put yourself in her shoes. You imagine what it must be like for her. That's what good friends do, right? You see how hopeless the situation is. Even if you come up with some solutions, she's quick to point out why they won't work. You begin to feel what she feels. You are lowering your vibration to match hers.

It's important to note that this has nothing to do with her. She cannot force you to lower your vibration. No one can. You have to let it happen. Not letting it happen is, of course, much easier when you're consciously aware of what's going on. So, now that you know what's happening on an energetic level, what can you do the next time your friend comes around to complain?

One solution, of course, is to just stop talking to her. Now, generally this isn't a great option since it won't always be possible to get away from lower frequency people and learning how to stabilize your vibration will protect you in all situations. However, sometimes you need to get away from the energy drain for a bit in order to stabilize.

This applies to geographic locations as well. You might have a hard time stabilizing your vibration in a certain city or country, for example, or you might not be strong enough to raise your vibration while in a certain job. It's entirely possible to return to that location or company at a later time, once you're stronger, and not be effected by it anymore.

Let's assume that cutting your friend out of your life is not really an option. Here's an advise: Refuse to play in her playground with her. You are going to consciously hold on to your good feeling vibration. And if she wants to play with you in your higher, yummy, optimistic playground, then she has to join you where you are.

You're not going to come to her playground of misery and despair. Make no mistake - this will take discipline. And if your friend is used to you commiserating with her, she will most likely react badly to the change at first. Persevere. This does not mean that you have to be fake-happy. Just be who you are and stay there.

Here are some options:

1. Change the subject. When she begins to complain about her boss, tell her that you'd really like to talk about something else. You know that she really wants to feel better, and you think that it'll be much easier to accomplish that if you both focus on a happy subject. Explain that beating the drum of how horrible her job is just ends up making you both feel badly.

2. Keep turning the subject around. If she talks about her jerk of a boss, ask her if he's always a jerk, or just

sometimes. Does he have any redeeming qualities at all? Try to get her to focus on that. Yes, this will annoy her at first. She wants to complain to you and she wants you to join her so she can feel validated. But you're going to refuse to join her - for your sake. Remember that she's used to you lowering your vibration to meet hers. If you suddenly refuse, she will either need to raise her vibration to meet yours or get away from you. The vibrational discord between you will be too uncomfortable. You have to become a match, or split. And if you refuse to budge, she will have to. Or she'll walk away. If that's the case, let it happen.

3. Do not see your friend as helpless and stuck. She is not. She may currently think that she is, but she's just as powerful as being as you are. And you cannot force her to realize it any more than she can force you to lower your vibration. But know that when you do lower your energy to match hers - you are in no way helping her. The only true way to help her is keep

holding your vibration and give her the chance to come up and meet you.

4. Find something YOU can feel good about in the conversation and focus on it. You are not actively trying to get her to raise her vibration. That's not your job. Your goal is stay where you are. So even if you listen to her saga, translate all of it into a perspective that you can feel good about.

5. Walk away. If the situation becomes too uncomfortable for you (neither one of you is budging), make an excuse and walk away. You are not abandoning her. If she can't hear you, can't come up to meet your vibration, and you know that you cannot help her by lowering your vibration, then you have to take a break. This may happen the first couple of times. Remember that she is used to you behaving one way, and probably won't react well to the sudden change. But you can't help anyone from a place of low

vibration, so protecting your own frequency has to come first.

6. Practice this technique with strangers at first - it will be most difficult to use with people you care a great deal about. You don't have to become cold or uncaring; you don't have to become hostile or fake happiness. You can still be loving and compassionate (more so in fact, when your vibration stays high), you can still help people. Just refuse to let others determine how you feel.

This will take a bit of work. It might even take a lifetime to learn how to hold your vibration in ALL situations. Even people who have incredibly stable vibrations would have a hard time walking into a warzone and staying happy and at peace. This is why you shouldn't be afraid to remove yourself from a situation that makes it impossible for you to stabilize. The rest, however, can be conquered with a bit of perseverance and practice.

CHAPTER 5

TOOLS FOR AN EMPATH'S ENERGY PROTECTION

Common traits of an Empath and why they need protection:

Empaths are drawn to healing themselves and others. They are usually drawn to healing, because they feel that they have so much internal healing to do... until, that is, they realize that most of the healing needed is for others that they are intuitively 'feeling'.

They are usually in a state of constant fatigue. This is a huge issue. People, along with their energies are constantly invading an Empath's energy. An Empath will usually take on too much and become drained very quickly, and it's not easily cured by sleep or rest. It goes much deeper than that and is quite exhausting.

Empaths are excellent listeners. They genuinely care about the well-being of others and find themselves listening to the woes of people they don't even know. Most people find Empaths so easy to open up to. That's when they start dumping all kinds of negativity going in their life. Sometimes, people aren't even aware they are doing this.

In most cases, an Empath with take care of the needs of others even before their own, because they care so much. Since people get comfortable enough around them to open up, they will usually selflessly lend their ear to help a person; even if it's to their own detriment.

Alone time is a necessity for an Empaths. Many Empaths like to get away from all of the emotions and energy that is not theirs so they require much needed time alone. This is time for them to get back to balance, and distance themselves from all negativity that is not theirs.

An Empath can also appear as moody. Empaths sometimes seem to have major mood swings, and this sometimes is contributed to all of the overwhelming thoughts and feelings bombarding them on a daily basis. Not only are they bombarded with these energies, but now they need to clearly sort through and figure out all that stuff coming their way.

They are emotionally sensitive to violence, cruelty, or any sort of tragedy. Most Empaths quit watching the television and reading the newspapers at some point in their lives, as this too, can be very overwhelming for an empath.

Just plain knowing is also a common Empath trait. Empaths sometimes know things that they are positive they were never taught or told. This knowing is very different than intuition or a gut feeling.

Being in public places is often overwhelming or painful to an empath. Again so many people's emotions are in public places that can be picked up when not even trying to. This is a roller coaster most Empaths will avoid at all costs.

An Empath can 'feel' honesty and integrity. They can tell if someone is being honest or not, which is very unsettling and sometimes painful in your life. It's especially unsettling when they are dealing with loved ones.

Feeling the physical symptoms and pains of another. Many Empaths will find themselves developing an ailment that someone else has that has nothing to do with them. This is empathy at its finest.

These are just a few of the traits of an Empath. Again, being an Empath can be either considered a curse or a gift depending on the tools you use to protect yourself. There are many ways for Empaths to protect themselves. Avoiding large social gatherings or public places at all costs is one way. But there are times when you just cannot avoid these things. There are quite a few helpful ways to protect yourself as an empath.

CRYSTALS

- Rose Quartz is a fantastic crystal for an Empath because its healing properties promote unconditional love and comfort. This is especially good for a person that may be holding less than loving energies of something, someone, or even themselves.

- Black Tourmaline or Hematite are also great crystals for an Empath to help them stay grounded. These stones will also help to absorb any negative energies.

- Malachite is another crystal that will help absorb any negative feelings you may be having; whether they are your own or not!

- Labradorite is a crystal that will actually help protect your aura from absorbing any issues that are being shared with you.

- Citrine is a yellow crystal to help brighten your mood. Another Citrine healing property is that it can also help absorb bad energy from your environment.

- Another go to crystal for me is Amethyst. Not only is it beautiful, but it will strengthen your intuition. Heightened intuition is wonderful for everyone, but especially for Empaths to help them truly know that the feelings they may be having are theirs or not.

- Last but not least is Rainbow Fluorite. Rainbow Fluorite may very well be, in my opinion, the Mother of all crystals for an Empath as it helps all levels of being! This is a multi-colored crystal that can help you stay grounded to the earth, help clear and balance all Chakras, as well as to help you stay attuned to higher dimensions.

MEDITATION

Meditation has been used for thousands of years as a way to attain a level of awareness that is beyond the limitations of the everyday thinking mind. Quite simply, it's the practice of bringing together, the mind, body, and spirit!

Most don't realize that our bodies were meant to be self-correcting to maintain positive health by simply keeping mind, body and spirit in balance. Imagine how easy it is to be out of balance when the energy of others infiltrates your body on a daily basis. It's epic!

When you're out of balance, your life-force energy doesn't flow quite the way it should. Being out of balance shows up in life as aches and pains. And when you're out of balance for long enough, your body begins to create illness and disease.

Alone time and meditation is a wonderful way for an empath to keep themselves balanced, healthy and whole. This is the practice of loving yourself that most Empaths put at the back of the line, if they even put it in the line of importance at all!

CRYSTALS FOR EMPATHS

Most empathic children have a special connection to nature, and this is because nature helps us to find solitude, disconnect and recharge, and the negative ions we receive from touching the earth help balance our energy bodies and emotions. Crystals can be a fun, and concrete way to help your empathic child feel safe, strengthen their bond with nature, and utilize the energetic properties of crystals to support their gifts.

One of the beautiful things about children, especially empathic children, is that they are naturally intuitive and energetically sensitive. So most empathic children will naturally know which crystals they are drawn to, and form a relationship with each of their crystals, understanding which ones they need at which times in their lives. This is one of the ways you can help empower your empathic child through self-care: listening to their bodies, and their intuition, to know what they need in each moment.

I usually will suggest that parents take their child to a local crystal or metaphysical store, and let their child pick out the crystals that speak to them – and yes, many children literally do speak to their crystals, just as you or I might speak to a friend and confidant. It's a fun game to play with your child, to see what crystals they are drawn to, and then ask the salesperson or read up on the properties of the crystal afterward. As your child is getting to know his/her crystals, you may ask them what they feel from each crystal, if the crystal has a name (or if they'd like to give it one), where the crystal wants to be in their room, etc. Depending on size and safety of the crystal, I have several children who sleep with their crystals, holding them in their hands, or set up a crystal grid on their nightstand to help them feel safe. Some great crystals to consider for empathic children

Are:

• Black Tourmaline - A very widely known stone of protection is Black Tourmaline.

Commonly used by Crystal-Healers, Black Tourmaline is a great ally for those exposed to negative energies regularly. It can protect you against electromagnetic smog and debilitating diseases. Black Tourmaline helps to clear the aura and surrounding environment of negative vibrations. It can be very helpful during these changing times, and is supportive of the vibrational shift that the planet is currently undergoing. Black Tourmaline helps to balance all of the subtle energy bodies with the physical, encouraging a harmony of vibration which in turns, can facilitate a greater flow in our lives. Specifically,Black Tourmaline can protect against psychic attacks, negative entities, and psychic debris.

• **Hematite** - Hematite helps to absorb negative energy and calms you in times of stress or worry. Hematite is a very protective stone, and is great to carry to help you stay grounded in many situations. Hematite can boost confidence, and is also good for working with the

• **Obsidian** - Black Obsidian Stone is a powerful cleanser of psychic smog created within your aura, and is a strong psychic protection stone. It has powerful metaphysical properties that will shield you against negativity, and the energy of these stones may stimulate the gift of prophecy. Pieces of these stones that had a shiny surface were used in the past as a tool for scrying. It an excellent crystal to use when you have been doing spiritual or healing work... as it has a strong action to ground you to Mother Gaia. This black stone is excellent to assist you to release disharmony that has built up in your day to day life and during work on yourself, including resentment of others, fear and anger.

• **Selenite** - A protective stone, Selenite shields a person or space from outside influences.

Selenite can evoke protection from the angelic realm and also dispels negative energy.

Selenite calms and brings deep peace, and offers access to past and future lives. Selenite brings mental clarity, clearing confusion and revealing the bigger picture behind problems.

Use Selenite in a grid around your home or in the corners of a room to create a safe and peaceful space. Selenite also removes energy blocks from physical and etheric bodies.

Selenite is said to reverse the effects of "free radicals" to heal and repair on the cellular level.

• **Amethyst** - Amethyst is a spiritually protective crystal, possessing a high vibration that helps to strengthen the aura against negative energies. It carries a serene vibration that helps one to remain calm in the face of any adverse situations, and also stimulate energies to rise in response to a problem or threat. Amethyst can work to protect one from the self by elevating and balancing mood, and by removing anger and frustration to be replaced by peace and selflessness. This raising of one's own personal vibration has a tendency to attract higher experiences to the self, repelling the negative ones. Keeping an Amethyst

Cluster in one's home or office can protect the space from negative energies coming in, and emit a higher vibration, allowing for a greater connection to the spiritual realms. Amethyst also protects astral travelers from negative entities trying to attach themselves to one's energy field. Protecting against all forms of psychic attack, Amethyst facilitates a connection to the Divine by activating the Third-Eye and Crown Chakras.